An Adults Only Guide to Getting E-Rich

While every precaution has been taken in the preparation of this book, the publisher assumes no responsibility for errors or omissions, or for damages resulting from the use of the information contained herein.

AN ADULTS ONLY GUIDE TO GETTING E-RICH

First edition. August 3, 2024.

Copyright © 2024 Sue D Onim.

ISBN: 979-8227581679

Written by Sue D Onim.

THIS PAGE INTENTIONALLY LEFT BLANK

Cam Site	Type	Average Monthly	Model Pay Range	Rev Share	Pay Frequency
Stripchat	Tokens & PPM	$11,580	$10,000 - $15,000	50 - 60%	Weekly
Xmodels	Pay-Per-Minute	$9,040	$5,500 - $12,000	45 - 75%	Bi-Weekly
Chaturbate	Tokens & PPM	$8,420	$4,000 - $20,000	60%	Weekly
Camsoda	Tokens Only	$6,890	$3,500 - $11,000	55%	Weekly
OnlyFans	Subscription	$5,340	$3,300 - $8,500	80%	Weekly
BongaCams	Tokens Only	$4,250	$3,000 - $8,000	60 - 90%	Bi-Weekly
LiveJasmin	Pay-Per-Minute	$3,970	$2,000 - $7,500	30 - 80%	Bi-Weekly
Streamate	Pay-Per-Minute	$3,350	$2,000 - $7,000	30%	Weekly
Flirt4Free	Pay-Per-Minute	$2,890	$2,000 - $6,500	20 - 30%	Bi-Weekly
Streamray	Pay-Per-Minute	$2,660	$1,500 - $6,000	32 - 70%	Bi-Weekly

A cam girl, also known as a webcam model, earns money by performing and offering adult services online. The webcam industry has seen tremendous growth and demand over the past few years, leading many women to pursue it as a career. If you're one of those women eager to learn how to become a cam girl, this comprehensive guide is for you. We'll cover everything from setting up your space and the essential equipment you'll need, to quickly earning money from your shows and tips on additional revenue streams.

I've compiled a data-driven guide to help you succeed in this industry. While the structure may seem eclectic, the information is both relevant and practical.

Whether you're a first-time cam girl or an experienced adult modeling professional aiming to elevate your camming career, the resources and statistics in this guide will reveal the proven strategies used by the world's most successful and highest-earning cam girls.

WHAT IS A CAM GIRL & WHAT IS CAM MODELING?

A cam girl, or webcam model, performs services like dancing, stripping, and sex- and fetish- related activities for her fans in front of a webcam. Their performance is broadcasted live from a camera connected to a computer or laptop to the camming site she broadcasts on.

Customers or viewers can watch the cam girl on her page, chat with her, and tip her money to do something specific or activity the cam girl offers.

A girl that has chosen to make money camming has to build a unique relationship with

the fans on her channel by understanding their needs and desires and providing them with exactly what they are ready to pay for. Whether you wish to become a webcam girl because you have heard about the amazing income or you enjoy the activities of camming, you will need to do your own research and learn everything there is if you wish to be successful and stand out among all the webcam models out there.

Becoming a Cam Girl

To make money on webcam, you will first need to decide what you want to achieve. Do you want to make a little money on the side until or if you wish to turn it into your full-time job?

Do you want to be a cam girl for a short period of time or do you want to be really dedicated to it and turn it into your career?

Whatever you do, don't dive into this world without deciding on a persona you want to adopt for your clients. Not only will this affect your success, but it will also ensure you enjoy your work and have fun along the way.

After all, this is just like any other job out there. You wouldn't start working in an industry you have zero knowledge of, so why should it be any different with camming? In other words, it's not just about how to become a cam girl, it's about understanding how YOU want to connect with your future fans.

These are some questions you should ask yourself before you sign up on a cam site:

- Do I see myself doing this short-term or long-term?
- How many hours would I like to dedicate to this?
- What type of cam girl persona goes well with my personality?
- Do I feel comfortable doing this?
- Which things are on my "OFF-LIMITS" list?
- What makes me different from all the other cam girls out there?

This list of questions should determine where you see yourself in the camming world and what your goals are. Keep in mind that you can easily change your mind after you've been performing for your fans for a while, but understanding what you want in the beginning will save you from many headaches in the future.

How Much Money Do Cam Models Make?

Let's be real for a second. You probably want to become a cam model because you've heard the money is good. And there's no doubt about it - it really is! However, not everyone earns the same amount of money, and being a beginner you shouldn't expect to earn as much as a cam girl with years of experience.

The income of almost every cam girl will increase with time as she gains more exposure, and exposure will increase the number of new customers and old customers who become repeat customers. With experience comes the opportunity to leverage new streams of making money. So, the question of how to become a cam girl also involves how you can make money through other streams with your cam girl status. You could become a cam girl that makes videos that attract a new and existing audience and turn your page into a must- visit space in the camming world.

These are some factors that will impact your earnings as a cam girl:

- **Your age**: Younger girls will earn more money than the girls in their 40s.
- **Level of experience**: Beginners may not earn as much money as

cam girls with several years of experience. However, there are plenty of exceptions.

- **Cam website**: The audience is different on each cam site, from their spending habits to their preferences.
- **Additional streams of income**: Cam girls who have multiple streams of income will earn more than those relying solely on their cam site performance.

If you're just starting out, don't expect to make $10,000 per month. Yes, there are several articles that state some models make $50,000 - $100,000 per month, but keep in mind that it took most of these girls years and years to build their career and turn it into a profitable full-time job. But, to give you an idea of your potential earnings, a beginner cam girl can expect to earn around $200 per day on average if she works 3-5 hours a day.

Another thing you should keep in mind when asking yourself, "How much do cam girls make?" is a lack of financial stability. Some days you will earn a solid income and some days, you may struggle to even earn just a couple of dollars. There may not be much stability when it comes to camming, so it's best that you are prepared for bad days. Keep in mind that most camming websites will take a commission at around 35%, so it's important to understand the difference between the total amount your camming sessions bring in vs. your take-home pay.

What's it Like to Be a Cam Girl?

Curious to find out what your life will look like once you become a cam girl? Well, becoming a cam girl means you will have to be prepared for the unexpected, consider your financial situation, invest in good equipment and outfits, follow the trends of the industry, and also find your niche. Most cam girls out there continue living their everyday life - hanging out with their friends and family, picking up new hobbies, traveling and exploring the world, etc.

After you decide how many hours you want and need to work, your lifestyle will depend on how much time you choose to put into camming. If you become successful and camming becomes your only source of income, you'll have more time to enjoy other activities in your life that will help you become more creative and attentive to your audience's needs. So, the question is not really "how to be a cam girl", but how you can truly prepare before you

start camming to be fully ready for whatever this new adventure might bring you!

Getting Started With Cam Modeling

If after reading this, you are even more determined and eager to become a part of

the camming world and create video content and have live performances which will provide you with a decent income, start looking for a cam site to sign up on. Don't forget that your activities don't have to be limited to that particular website. There is an endless number of income opportunities waiting for you!

You can also develop a camgirl starter pack which will consist of various supporting activities, such as your social media profiles, affiliate marketing, etc. These starter packs are a fantastic idea if you want to create a strong connection with your audience and expand your influence across several platforms.

So, now that you know how to become a cam girl and how to make money as a cam girl, start exploring camming websites while thinking about the type of cam girl you want to be. In our exhaustive cam girl guide, you will find all the tips you need to become successful in this realm and create an online presence that people will be interested in!

Are you curious about becoming a webcam model? Want to know which cam sites are the best to work for and which cam site will make you the most money?

You came to the right place!

This guide will teach you everything you need to pick the right cam site to start out with, and show you how to maximize your earnings as a webcam model.

Scraping data from teams of professional webcam models spent over 18 months testing out every major cam site and meticulously scoring them to determine which cam site is best and consistently pays the most, and here we are. Passion meets discipline.

Testing over 80 different sites, we scored each cam site based on best and highest-paying viewer audience, ease of use, most fun for broadcasters, best overall experience for models, and most importantly, which cam site produced the most take home earnings with the least amount of effort and time required.

From the 80+ cam sites we tested, we narrowed it down to the top 10 best cam sites for models to make money camming, and ranked them below.

These 10 cam sites are truly the best choices for aspiring cam girls. If you want to learn how to become a webcam model and maximize your earnings from camming, read on below to see which cam girl sites scored the best!

Cam Site	Type	Average Monthly	Model Pay Range	Rev Share	Pay Frequency
Stripchat	Tokens & PPM	$11,580	$10,000 - $15,000	50 - 60%	Weekly
Xmodels	Pay-Per-Minute	$9,040	$5,500 - $12,000	45 - 75%	Bi-Weekly
Chaturbate	Tokens & PPM	$8,420	$4,000 - $20,000	60%	Weekly
Camsoda	Tokens Only	$6,890	$3,500 - $11,000	55%	Weekly
OnlyFans	Subscription	$5,340	$3,300 - $8,500	80%	Weekly
BongaCams	Tokens Only	$4,250	$3,000 - $8,000	60 - 90%	Bi-Weekly
LiveJasmin	Pay-Per-Minute	$3,970	$2,000 - $7,500	30 - 80%	Bi-Weekly
Streamate	Pay-Per-Minute	$3,350	$2,000 - $7,000	30%	Weekly
Flirt4Free	Pay-Per-Minute	$2,890	$2,000 - $6,500	20 - 30%	Bi-Weekly
Streamray	Pay-Per-Minute	$2,660	$1,500 - $6,000	32 - 70%	Bi-Weekly

Success stories from the camming industry

Like any profession, webcam modeling has its rockstar earners and celebrity-level personalities. While doing the supporting research for this article, our team came across some nice examples of already publicly available success stories in the industry. Want to know how much some of these cam girls earn on the best camming sites?

- Jessie Lee - $240,000 per year
- Lola-Rose Curtis - $191,000 per year
- Clara Joy - $96,000 per year
- Jayme Jones - $66,000 per year
- Cecilia Renee Morrell - $36,000 per year.

Similar to what we covered above, the main reason these numbers vary so much from person to person is due to working hours. Keep in mind that cam models rarely work a full eight-hour shift. The majority of them work four or five hours per day, and may not even work all the days of the week. Of course, becoming popular in the camming world will positively affect your income but as a beginner, it would be wiser to stick to the "more hours, more money" formula.

How Do You Earn Your First Paycheck?

In order to get paid, you will need to know the rules of your chosen cam site. Some of the best cam girl sites might seem too good to be true when you're doing research, but that's only because you may not have considered the commission rate. That is how the system works - you charge for a service you've provided on the website, and that website takes a commission for your service.

Usually, the commission ranges from 40 to 50%, but make sure to check that detail before signing up on a site. After all, it will have a tremendous impact on your earnings. Once

a webcam girl signs up on a cam site, she is expected to set up her payment details. You should provide your bank account details or other payment details and ensure this method is approved by the website.

Once your account has been verified, you will be able to start your first live show and earn money. However, setting up your prices is vital before you dive into all of this. A good piece of advice would be to talk to or watch other camgirls to find out how much they charge and what works best for them.

How to Choose the Best Webcam for Streaming

Without a good camera, you can't expect to make money and have a high-quality show. All the popular cam girls you see out there, whether it's on YouTube or any webcam site, have invested money into their camming equipment first so they can engage their fans and provide them with a top-notch cam site experience. So, the next step for you is to find the best webcam for streaming.

Luckily, the equipment you will need will be a worthwhile investment. When you consider your future income, you will see it's just a one-off expense you will need to cover. When it comes to your webcam equipment, these are several technical factors that will have a great impact on your success.

In this chapter, we'll provide you with all the information you need to know before you go shopping for camming equipment. With our tips, your cam experience will be exactly how you pictured it to be - perfect!

LAPTOP

Some cam girls use their laptop's built-in camera to stream their show. The reasons for this are very simple - it's easy to use and doesn't require you to purchase a separate webcam. During your performance, you don't have to worry about holding the camera or changing up your lighting or angles.

Here is a list of **laptops with the best webcams**:

- 13-inch MacBook Air ($999 USD - $1,299 USD)
- HP x360 Convertible 2-in-1 Chromebook ($329 USD - $499 USD)
- Lenovo Yoga C930 2-in-1 13.9 ($988 USD - $1199 USD)
- Samsung Galaxy 13.3 4K Ultra HD Touch Screen ($718 USD - $999 USD)

Purchasing a new laptop may be the best first step if you don't have a good quality laptop.

EXTERNAL WEBCAM

Your camgirl career can start with nothing more than a basic webcam that offers a 720p HD video. This would be enough to ensure you're providing your fans with a high-quality experience. If you want to up your budget to improve image quality, you can consider 4K Ultra HD videos. Cameras with a good zoom, slow motion options, and great audio input are just some of the features you will get if you purchase a good webcam.

If you know nothing about webcam technology, don't panic. We've done the research for you and have compiled a list of **the best webcams on the market:**

- High Definition C922X Logitech Webcam ($99.99 USD)
- Logitech Super Clear C270 High Quality Webcam ($53.50 USD)
- Logitech Extra Superb C310 Fine Webcam ($49.99 USD)
- Digital Wireless Dropcam Camera ($200 USD)
- High Definition 3000 Powerful MS LifeCam ($39.95USD - $139.67 USD)

If none of the above are what you consider being the best camera for streaming, please make sure you pay attention to the following when buying a new webcam:

- **Resolution** - No lower than 720p
- **Megapixels** - Between 5MP and 15MP
- **Weight** - Below 270g

PHONE

Don't have the money to purchase a new camera or a laptop? Don't worry, plenty of streaming sites now offer the option to stream from your mobile. Not to say that having a quality webcam is not beneficial for every cam girl, but if you're not able to spend money on camming equipment at the moment, you can test out streaming on your phone.

So, here's how to use phone as webcam and not worry about the lighting, angles, and everything else that might affect your streamed shows. Whether you're using an Android phone, iPhone, or iPad for your camera, there are several apps that can improve your streaming quality. Luckily, most of them are affordable and you can easily find the best one for the model of your phone.

You can directly use your phone camera to stream, but as it might be complicated to hold your phone for your entire performance, most cam girls purchase a tripod. You can find a good tripod at almost any store that sells electronics or on Amazon for a reasonable price.

As a guideline, a fair quality tripod will be priced anywhere from $70 - $200 USD. If you can't afford a new laptop or a webcam, 70 dollars for a good tripod won't break the bank. And, don't worry about the impact a phone camera will have on your first few performances.

Camming Set Up Tips for the Best Cam Girl Room

Once you have purchased the equipment you will be using for your camming set up and created your profile on the website, it's time to turn your focus to your work environment! You will likely work from the comfort of your bedroom as it will provide you

with the right space and freedom to perform and make successful webcam videos. Using your own room instead of a studio will save you a lot of money as the renting prices can be high.

So, how can you convert your room into a webcam studio? There are numerous ways to do this, from altering your bedroom layout to recording in a dedicated camming room in your home. As the majority of webcam girls use their bedrooms, especially at the beginning of their careers, we'll focus solely on how to set up your cam area in your bedroom.

Some questions you might have may include: What are the essential features you need to get high-quality videos? Where should you position your purchased equipment to ensure your viewers are getting the value they deserve? Here are all the tips you need to set up your cam space.

1. Stripchat - Best Overall

Stripchat is #1 on the list for one simple reason: highest **average** model earnings.

Of all the cam sites we've tested, Stripchat gives the most take-home pay to the average model, due to a nice mixture of high traffic, viewers who are accustomed to spending big through pay-per-minute private and exclusive chats, and a high percentage of earnings that the model gets to keep.

Stripchat is a great choice for new models that need to earn as much as possible in their first few weeks. The site offers up to 60% rev share to models, and has a special feature where **new models get boosted site placement for 2 weeks** to help you get established and earn real money in your first few weeks.

The downside of Stripchat is that the viewer community expects to see mostly freemium shows and to pay models via tips. This can be great for models who know how to earn tips, and for the best models can result in even higher earnings than pay-per-minute private and exclusive chat sites, but you should research how to maximize tips in your cam show before you start to make sure you get the most out of your initial 2 week boosted placement.

That said, Stripchat does also offer Private Shows, Cam2Cam Shows and Spy Shows where you can get paid by the minute and get to set your own price, which is a huge plus.

The best strategy on Stripchat is to attract viewers in your freemium show, and then entice them into taking you private where you'll get paid by the minute at whatever price you set. With this strategy, your earnings on Stripchat are nearly unlimited.

Stripchat also has nice modern technology that's easy to use, as well as good privacy controls for the model and contests that pay out an extra $20,000 to models each month. Lastly, an important note is that Stripchat broadcasts your show to both Stripchat.com and XhamsterLive.com, which doubles the viewership and makes the total audience competitive with Chaturbate.

Stripchat is simply the best site for most beginner camgirls and we recommend it as the #1 choice for any webcam model who is just getting started and wants maximize their earnings.

Stripchat at a glance:

- Type: Tokens & pay-per-minute private chats
- Monthly traffic: 119,670,000 viewers (Stripchat)
- Monthly traffic: 142,240,000 viewers (XHamsterLive)
- Average model pay: $9,580 / mo
- Range of model pay: $8,000 - $15,000 / mo
- Percent of revenue model keeps: 50 - 60%
- Payout frequency: Weekly

2. Xmodels

Xmodels can be a great choice for models who want to build up a stable source of income they can depend on for a long time.

Some cam sites keep as much as 70-75% of your earnings for themselves, meaning you get to keep only a fraction of what you earn. Xmodels is much better, with the site only taking 25-50%, so you can get double or triple the take-home-pay through Xmodels.

While Xmodels is based in Europe and is the #1 cam site in Europe, models from anywhere in the world can sign up. In fact, many of the top earning models on Xmodels are from the United States. What's great about the European audience of Xmodels is that you get viewers from many rich countries like Switzerland and Norway who are willing to pay a lot for a private show with you, and additionally, if you live in the United States, you're much less likely to get seen by a friend or family member that you know browsing the site.

Lastly, a very important note about Xmodels is that you must cam on the site for 100 hours before you will be allowed to set your own price for private and exclusive chats. The

initial per-minute rate is low, so it's hard to make significant earnings until you've reached that 100 hour threshold and can raise your price. So keep this in mind and don't get discouraged initially. We recommend trying to power through your first 100 hours of camming as quickly as possible to unlock the ability to raise your prices. Once you can set your own prices, the earnings from Xmodels are fantastic.

Overall, we recommend giving Xmodels a try, especially if you want to invest in becoming a webcam model as a long-term profession.

Xmodels at a glance:

- Type: pay-per-minute private chats
- Monthly traffic: 636,000 viewers
- Average model pay: $7,040 / mo
- Range of model pay: $4,500 - $12,000 / mo
- Percent of revenue model keeps: 45 - 75%
- Payout frequency: Every 2 weeks

3. Chaturbate - Highest Earnings Potential

Chaturbate is the largest cam site in the world by traffic, with over 300 million monthly visitors. It's also the fastest cam site with the most robust technology.

Chaturbate is a great cam site to work for, but it is more competitive than Xmodels. Chaturbate has more models than any other cam site, meaning you have to be a top performer to do really well.

The best models on Chaturbate make huge amounts of money, with some models raking in over $1 million per year, and a large number of models earning at least $20,000 per month. However, since Chaturbate is so competitive, the average Chaturbate model actually earns less than the average model on Xmodels, which is why we ranked in #2.

The key question to ask yourself when deciding whether Chaturbate is right for you is whether you feel you can entertain a room full of people, vs. performing in 1-on-1 or more intimate chats. To maximize your earnings on Chaturbate, you will need to be able to entertain a large audience all at once.

Another nice benefit of Chaturbate is that you get to keep 60% of your earnings, which is high compared to most cam sites, and they pay out weekly, so you can start getting paid rather quickly.

Overall, we recommend Chaturbate if you want to absolutely maximize your earnings potential and are willing to dedicate the time and energy to become a top performer on the site.

Chaturbate at a glance:

- Type: Tokens & pay-per-minute private chats
- Monthly traffic: 320,840,000 viewers
- Average model pay: $6,420 / mo
- Range of model pay: $3,000 - $20,000 / mo
- Percent of revenue model keeps: 60%
- Payout frequency: Weekly

4. Camsoda - Best For Instant Earnings

Camsoda is a relatively high traffic cam site with good a revenue share for models. Performers on Camsoda get to keep 55% of their earnings, which is a better than most cam sites. Despite this, Camsoda is lower in our list because of the viewer audience. Most viewers on Camsoda are there to see free shows, and only a small handful want to tip. Top Camsoda models can still earn a good amount from camming, but it's harder than on other cam sites.

Where Camsoda really shines is for models who want to use their cam site to also drive sales of photos and videos. The top Camsoda models actually make more money from selling photos and videos to viewers than they do from the tips they receive directly from actual camming.

If you want to sell photos and videos in addition to camming, Camsoda could be a good choice for you.

Camsoda at a glance:

- Type: tokens + sell photo & videos
- Monthly traffic: 66,480,000 viewers
- Average model pay: $5,890 / mo
- Range of model pay: $3,500 - $11,000 / mo
- Percent of revenue model keeps: 55%
- Payout frequency: Weekly

5. OnlyFans - Best Automatic Subscription

OnlyFans is not a cam site, it's actually a paid, subscriber-only social media platform. It's just like an Instagram or Twitter account, except your followers have to pay you a monthly subscription fee in order to view your posts and feed. You set the price of the subscription (typically $5 - $30 / month per follower). OnlyFans takes a 20%, and the remaining 80% of the subscription fee goes to you.

Though it's not technically a camming site, we included OnlyFans in the list because it's an amazing way for most webcam models to earn extra money, and the fact that it pays you monthly subscription revenue (regardless of how much time you spend on it) can be a great supplement to your income.

If you want to become a cam girl, definitely consider also starting an OnlyFans account to get an extra stable income stream coming in, month after month, even when you're not working or on vacation. Many cam models also drive viewers that they interact with on the other cam sites to their OnlyFans profile as a way of getting more subscribers on OnlyFans.

OnlyFans at a glance:

- Type: subscription
- Monthly traffic: 83,190,000 viewers
- Average model pay: $4,340 / mo
- Range of model pay: $3,300 - $8,500 / mo
- Percent of revenue model keeps: 80%
- Payout frequency: Weekly

6. BongaCams - Highest Percentage Paid To Model

BongaCams is the 2nd largest cam girl site on the internet, with 310 million monthly visitors. It has extremely high traffic, which means the top models and earn a huge amount.

BongaCams is a good choice if you want to work for tips in a free show with very high traffic. It pays out the highest % of revenue to the model of any cam site online today. It generally has great reviews from the models who use it.

The one place BongaCams falls down is if you want to primarily do pay-per-minute private or exclusive chats. BongaCams is very public, and its features for supporting private and exclusive chat are not as good as other cam sites. Additionally, most viewers on BongaCams expect to see free shows and to be able to pay through tips rather than pay-per-minute.

BongaCams at a glance:

- Type: tokens only
- Monthly traffic: 343,330,000 viewers
- Average model pay: $4,250 / mo
- Range of model pay: $3,000 - $8,000 / mo
- Percent of revenue model keeps: 60 - 90%

7. LiveJasmin - Best For Double-Dipping

LiveJasmin claims to be the #1 webcam site in the world, but they are actually #3 by traffic (both Chaturbate and BongaCams are slightly larger). That said, LiveJasmin is clearly in the top 3, and of the top sites is definitely the best one for models.

Unlike the other super-high-traffic cam sites, LiveJasmin relies more on pay-per-minute private sessions than token-based tipping, which typically works out to more earnings for the average model. On top of that, LiveJasmin offers a greater percentage of earnings available for the model to take home, so LiveJasmin revenue for the model can be fairly good and competitive with other top cam girl sites.

One of the best features of LiveJasmin is that it allows cam-splitting, so you can broadcast to LiveJasmin at the same time you're broadcasting to other sites and "double-dip" with your earnings. For this reason, many models log onto LiveJasmin in a second browser tab and leave their LiveJasmin show on at the same time as they're camming on their primary site like Xmodels or Chaturbate. Being on 2 sites at the same time means more time earning big in pay-per-minute private & exclusive chats, and less time sitting around waiting.

Overall - it's a great site if you want to get maximum exposure and have very high traffic.

LiveJasmin at a glance:

- Type: tokens & pay-per-minute private chat
- Monthly traffic: 244,900,000 viewers
- Average model pay: $3.970 / mo
- Range of model pay: $2,000 - $7,500 / mo
- Percent of revenue model keeps: 30 - 80%
- Payout frequency: Every 2 weeks

8. Streamate - Best For Private & Exclusive

Streamate is one of the best cam sites out there and an excellent choice for any model who wants to do camming as a side thing for income but cares about keeping it super private and not having friends or family run into you.

Streamate has built up an excellent community of high-paying viewers, and almost every viewer expects to do everything in private or exclusive chats, so you never have to show yourself publicly if you don't want to. Additionally, Streamate has some of the best privacy settings, allowing you to precisely control who can see what. Many Streamate models set

their privacy settings so that only paying members of the site can discover and see them. Additionally, you can block viewers in certain geographies like your home state or city, so you don't have to worry about friends or family seeing you on there.

Despite the privacy, Streamate models can earn a lot of money because viewers on streamate are higher-end and willing to spend a lot for models they love.

We recommend Streamate for models who are newer to camming and want to dip their toes into making extra money through camming, while still having great control over their privacy.

- Type: Pay-per-minute private & exclusive chats
- Monthly traffic: 23,450,000 viewers
- Average model pay: $3,350 / mo
- Range of model pay: $2,000 - $7,000 / mo
- Percent of revenue model keeps: 30%
- Payout frequency: Weekly

9. Flirt4Free - Best Technology

Flirt4Free is a solid cam site with a medium level of traffic. Where it shines most is in its technology. The interface for both viewers/members and models is the best and most bleeding-edge in the camming industry.

Though Flirt4Free models typically make most of their earnings through pay-per-minute private chats, the sleek interface for viewers does a great job of promoting tipping (and large tips), so that ends up increasing earnings for models as well.

The downside of Flirt4Free is that the site keeps 70-80% of what viewers pay, and you only get 20-30%. In terms of take-home earnings, that's not as bad as it sounds for models, because viewers on Flirt4Free tend to be big spenders, so there's more total dollars to share in the first place.

Still - we don't think 20-30% is quite fair and wish Flirt4Free would share more of the earnings with the model. Overall, we wouldn't recommend Flirt4Free as your primary cam site.

10. Streamray - Longest Running Cam Site

Streamray has been operating cam girl sites for over 15 years. They own several high traffic websites to bring viewers to your show, including Cams.com and AdultFriendFinder.

We like Streamray because viewers expect to pay to see what they want, and expectations around kinkiness are fairly vanilla. They do a good job providing models with privacy control, and models have the ability to keep up to 70% of their earnings as take-home pay.

Overall, we'd recommend Streamray as another good secondary site to get extra money while you're broadcasting on your main site.

What are the best cam girl sites?

The top 3 most popular webcam modeling sites by traffic are Chaturbate, BongaCams and LiveJasmin. Each of these sites receives between 275,000,000 - 325,000,000 visits per month, while most other cam sites have between 10,000,000 - 50,000,000 visits per month. Because Chaturbate, BongaCams and LiveJasmin have such high traffic, they also have high competition with many models competing for these viewers. This competition can make it harder for beginner cam models to do well on those larger sites, so we recommend starting with a smaller site like Xmodels or Streamate.

How much do cam girls make?

Most webcam models earn between $2,000 to $8,000 per month. The biggest factor the how much a webcam model makes is the number of hours per week worked. Many cam models who come in on the lower end of earnings tend to work only 10 - 15 hours per week. The top earning models typically work 30 - 40 hours per week. Beyond number of hours worked, the second biggest factor is which cam site you use. A high paying site like Xmodels will allow you to keep between 45-75% of your gross earnings as take-home pay, while other sites like Streamate only allow you to keep 30% of what you earn.

How can I earn $1000 a day as a webcam model?

The best cam models do indeed earn $1000 per day or more. These are dedicated models who cam full-time and treat camming as a serious profession. The secret is to build up a base of loyal followers and repeat customers, and to come online at regularly scheduled times so your fans know when they can expect you to be on. There are many other tips and tricks you will learn over time as you get more experience camming, from how you dress, to how you set up your camming space, to what you do in your shows, to additional products you sell for extra sources of income. These are all covered in our complete How To Become A Cam Girl Guide.

What's the best webcam for streaming?

While you can get away with using the built-in webcam on your Macbook or PC laptop, you'll typically do better with a professional webcam specifically designed for streaming. There are several factors to consider when choosing the best webcam for streaming, including cost, resolution, focus, zoom and compatibility with your computer. You can usually find a good webcam that will do the job in the $50 - $100 range on Amazon. The best webcam brands are Logitec and Razer.

To become a top cam girl, you will need much more than your computer and a good webcam. More often, the factor affecting your success the most is the cam site you choose to work for. You will have to choose a good cam site that will grant you the desired benefits

- a satisfying income, wider audience, and security.

To choose the best cam site, you will first need to determine what is important to you. Some girls will look for a low cam site commission or will only want to work on highly secure platforms with a lot of transparency, while others will be drawn to the most popular websites, such as Chaturbate, without even considering alternative solutions.

That's why we've decided to gather all the information to help you make the most of your cam girl experience and show you how to use all the opportunities these sites offer for their members.

Token Sites

By signing up on a token website, such as Chaturbate or MyFreeCams, you will be expected to entertain an audience in front of your webcam and perform while your fans interact with you and tip you with tokens. Although these sites have private and group options, meaning only one person or a small number of the audience can see you, your primary form of income will likely be through public tips.

Token-site girls will be more personality-based and will lean towards a more mixed interaction - chatting and performance. When comparing token sites with private ones, income for cam girls is usually higher, especially for those who become successful through a niche or their personality and performance. It also needs to be emphasized that token sites will require more intensive work and may be more stressful for beginners.

Private Sites

If you decide to sign up on one of the private sites, such as Streamate or Live Jasmin, expect a platform that operates much differently. There, you will have to present yourself, be chosen by somebody, and then that person will take you into a private room at a fixed rate. As mentioned above, private sites are usually less stressful than token sites because your main objective is getting someone to take you private which can stabilize your income.

This also means that private sites may not earn you money as much as, for

instance, Chaturbate would. One of the main characteristics of private sites is that the emphasis is not placed as much on the cam girl's personality, so if you're a beginner who doesn't want to socialize as much, you should consider signing up on a private webcam site.

PRO TIP: For the beginning of your webcam modeling career, use private sites to learn and determine what you want to offer people looking for these services. Once you feel more comfortable in your role, you can switch to token sites and start making more money!

How Things Work on Cam Sites

When going through the list of cam girl sites, you need to keep the commission rate in mind. Don't be too easily seduced when you see a website offering you an unreal amount of money because most of the time this means their commission is quite high, sometimes even up to 50%. So, how do you choose the right site?

Let's be clear, one style doesn't fit all. That's why you will have to decide what is relevant to you and how you want to build your cam modeling career. To give you an idea of how things work on the majority of cam sites, we'll provide you with information about the two most popular webcam sites - Chaturbate and Myfreecams.

Ranking on Chaturbate is determined by the number of people in your room relative to the time you have spent online. However, you will not experience any long-term consequences on your rank when you have low-earning days as ranking is only conducted daily for those who are online. On MyFreeCams, girls performing on their webcams will experience more pressure, as their rank is determined by their income per hour over the past 60 days. So, if you are not earning money, your rank will fall, which will prevent you from earning a higher hourly income.

Neither of the sites above has to be the one you sign up to. That's why we have prepared a thorough Top 10 list where you can find the best cam sites that suit your interests and objectives.

How Cam Girls Get Paid

After finding the best cam site for you, the next question you'll probably ask is, "How will I get paid?" Knowing that commission on these sites can be high, you might have the idea to use other methods for external income. In reality, this type of payment may only make up a small percentage of overall earnings for the majority of your cam modeling career. The main reason for this is the cam sites often ban mentions of any type of external payment, but those who capitalize on promotion using social media like Twitter can become successful.

Cam websites will incentivize tipping through the site through immediate feedback options to prevent girls from earning their money off-site, but if you're eager to find methods of external income, you should consider options such as clip sites, gift cards, and encouraging fans to purchase gifts for you off wish lists.

When thinking about how to become a cam girl, take at least a week or two for your research and planning. Blindly signing up on a website without checking if it has

the feature you are looking to use to build your career might terminate it before it even starts.

Never Settle

If you're already active on one of the cam model sites, keep in mind that you can always stop working on that site and sign up on a different one. There are various reasons why cam models might not be satisfied with the platform they chose to work on. For instance, the number of members on the site may be low and therefore you can't earn an income that is sufficient for you. Another reason could be that you are unable to improve your rank even if you work extra hours and perform at your best, or, you find the features and format of another site more appealing.

Besides being stuck on a website you don't enjoy working on, you should never settle when it comes to your income either. Models with experience on webcams can make more money if they spend a little time thinking about additional services they can offer to the members of their audience.

Once your personality is recognized and you start gaining fans that regularly visit your page, it will be easier to recognize what your audience likes and the methods you can use to deliver it to them, and consequently make more money.

Start Right Away

If you've done your homework and you're ready to become a cam model, sign up on one of the best cam sites and start earning your first paycheck. Your income will likely not be as high as you want it to be (unless you're lucky!), but keep in mind that you are just starting out and you will need some time to start running your cam page like a boss, princess, or whatever your cam girl persona may be!

To help you get started, we've gathered some advice from experienced cam models. Grab a pen and write them down, we know you'll need them!

- Your income will not be stable, especially in the beginning. Try to set a monthly goal for your first few months that is significantly lower than the ones you will aim for after that period.

- Treat your initial experiences as learning lessons. You are still getting to know the industry and you have the right to make a mistake and change your mind if you don't like something.
- Always look for information about commission before signing up on a website. Everything might look perfect at first, but not understanding how much money you will actually make is a common problem for most camgirl beginners.
- Try to avoid revealing your personal information, especially when you are first starting out. Once you feel more comfortable with your fans, you can decide what you want to share with them and to what degree.

WHAT ARE THE BEST CAM GIRL NAMES?

Your cam girl name is the first thing people on these sites will know about you. That's why it is vital that it matches your cam girl persona and how you want your audience to view you. You have probably already noticed that there are many types of camming personas out there, so looking at some existing ones may give you an idea of the one you want to adopt.

You can also choose a cam name based on your personal preferences. If you've always loved a certain name or style, why not use this opportunity and present yourself with it? Or, you can even invent something or choose a unique name that's not very common. Your username, as well as the name you give yourself will represent your brand in the cam world. For example, looking at Novaruu, cam girl who made a name for herself and who everyone recognizes by her name.

It's perfectly fine if you wish to stick to your own name once you set up your profile on one of these sites. The options are limitless, but that doesn't mean you should choose just any name that pops into your head. Keep in mind that changing your name once your career takes off may affect your cam girl identity, so ensure to choose one you feel will represent you for the rest of your career.

If you need a little help getting your brain juices flowing, here's a list of the ten most sexy female names to seduce your viewers:

1. Brianna
2. Erika

3. Lexi
4. Brooke
5. Vanessa
6. April
7. Natalie
8. Jenna
9. Molly
10. Katie

MATCH YOUR NAME WITH YOUR CAMMING PERSONA

As mentioned above, one of the easiest ways to choose your name is to match it with your camming persona. However, if you're just getting started, you most likely haven't

decided on your camming persona. That's why it would be a good idea to think of these two elements as two sides of the same coin.

To understand how to become a cam girl, you should first take a look at the different types of cam girls out there. Looking through the sea of girls on these modeling sites, we've gathered for you the most popular cam girl types and everything you need to know about them to provide your audience with an authentic camming experience!

Asian Cam Girl

An Asian cam model is a subcategory of the foreign cam girl type. Most of the time, these models are of Asian, African, or South American origin and they attract an enormous number of viewers with their exotic appearance and culture. However, their performance will go beyond their looks, as they might implement these cultural characteristics to seduce their target audience and provide them with a unique experience.

Asian cam girls are one of the most popular types in the camming community. Most of these girls live in Asia, but a lot of them can be found in Europe and the United States. So, check out the main features of an Asian cam model to see if this is something you can identify with:

- Petite body
- Young, fresh, and natural face
- Cute, girly outfits
- Somewhat shy and private

Headless Cam Girl

If you've become concerned about your privacy after exploring camming sites, this cam girl type is for you. As the name implies, these girls never show their face to their viewers and share very little personal details about themselves. Many girls will create a persona that leads a completely different life than their own, and their chosen name will often emphasize the mysterious aspect of their performance. Here are some main characteristics of a headless cam girl:

- Doesn't show her face
- Terrific and recognizable body
- Builds mystery around the privacy of her appearance

"I Only Look At My Phone" Cam Girl

Seeing as there are more and more people visiting cam sites every day, the number of cam girl types also increases. After all, more viewers means a variety of different tastes. One type that is becoming increasingly popular these days is the type of cam girl that only looks at her phone. These girls ignore their viewers during their time online and focus solely on their phones, a persona that entices those who prefer a disconnected experience between the model and themselves.

But, to succeed in such a role, you will need to feel comfortable and confident. Although you might think ignoring people on your channel is a seamless feat, it's actually harder than you think. Your performance will have to be very convincing and sharp, and you must demonstrate that this is in fact your persona. This cam girl type is hyper-focused

on tokens and nothing else.

If you think this might be your type, check if you fill out all the criteria:

- Not interested in connecting with the audience
- Really focused and determined to achieve their goal, e.g. ignoring their viewers
- Possess a strong attitude which is easily noticeable by others

Single Cam Girl

"All the single ladies, all the single ladies"... If that's your anthem, the single cam girl is your category! These girls enjoy emphasizing their single status to appeal to a wider audience.

The reason why many webcam models choose this type is that there are a lot of viewers who enjoy the prospect of the girlfriend experience.

Here are some tips for you if you're considering becoming a "single cam girl":

- Show off your single relationship status
- Provide an intimate and authentic girlfriend experience
- Ensure you make enough time to dedicate yourself to your fans and pamper them with your attention

Cosplay Cam Girl

If low-key is definitely not a word you would use to describe yourself or your cam girl type, then you might like the cosplaying type! A cosplay cam girl adores flashy, luxury clothes and cool costumes, and her style is the one thing her fans love the most about her. She spends most of her income on costumes and loves showing them off when working.

Her target audience is viewers interested in tipping their tokens to see her dress up as new characters. A portion of the cosplay cam girl's tokens contribute to her cosplay fund to buy materials, props, or costumes for her shows. If dressing up and being creative is part of what you wanted for your camming persona, keep these things in mind:

- You may need to earn a lot to purchase outfits for your shows
- Your performances will be built around the items you have purchased or received
- Your camming space needs to fit your theme

CAM GIRL PROFILE IDEAS: SETTING UP YOUR PROFILE

Once you have decided which cam girl type you are and which cam model name will you give yourself, it's time to set up your profile on one of the best cam sites for you. The sign-up process on most of these websites is similar and doesn't require too much time.

Here is the information you will need to submit to start working as a cam girl on your chosen site:

1. **Username**: Your username might want to include your cam model name.
2. **Password**: We don't have to remind you how important your security and privacy on these sites are. Choose a strong password!
3. **Email address:** It would be best to create a new email address for your camming job.
4. **Date of birth**: You can provide your real date of birth when signing up or put down a fake age.
5. **Identity Documents**: All cam sites will require you to have a scan or high- quality photograph of your official ID and additional pictures for security.

Once you have been confirmed to work on the website, you can start setting up your profile. If you're uncertain what information you need to include in your profile, you can always check out other girls' profiles to get an idea. We would advise you to have a clear profile with these elements:

- **Photo**: Choose a photo that will represent your cam girl persona.
- **Theme:** Ensure the theme and colors of your profile match your persona.
- **About**: Write about the experience you will give to your fans, your hobbies and preferences. If there's something that makes you different from all the other girls out there, make sure you add it to your profile.
- **Social media**: If you're looking to expand your audience and gain a following, you should link your social media channels and aim to boost your traffic on all of your platforms. (TIP: Create separate social media profiles just for your cam activities)
- **Schedule**: Girls from all around the world work on these sites, so be clear about the hours and time zone you will be online to your fans.

COMMON OOPS! MOMENTS

Although all this information seems straightforward, you should be sure of your cam model name, category, and brand before you set up your profile. Let's say you

start working under the name 'Shy Lucy' and you've chosen the single cam girl type. After a few months, you want to change your name and switch to the cosplay category. At this point, you may have already built up an audience, and changing your persona might lead to a lot of your fans leaving your page and messing up your rank position or reputation.

Doing your webcam videos all over again may not be an enjoyable process, so it's important to do it right the first time. Be clear about what type of experience you want to create for your audience and how you want to deliver it to them. Once you are 100% sure you know what you are doing, go for it!

Don't compare yourself to other girls as everyone is different. Some might enjoy publicity a lot more than you do, some may be more out there and extroverted, just make sure you know what you want before you press the stream button and go live on one of

these websites!

How to Get Tips and Make Money In Private Chat

The primary goal of every cam girl is to attract viewers to her page and bring a returning audience together to turn camming into a profitable career. However, achieving that is often not easy. You will need to focus on activities that can accumulate a good income such as paid private shows and continue engaging viewers on other platforms and in other ways.

Being a webcam girl is more than just performing in front of your audience, it involves profiting off of your online persona and skills which can earn you a solid income if you do things right.

Many cam sites provide you the opportunity to communicate with your fans on a more personal level in the form of paid private chats or shows. But how can you entice your fans to go into private chats or shows with you? When is the right time to take your interaction to a more personal environment and what do you do once you get there?

We've looked into the experiences of the most successful girls to provide you with useful tips and tricks that you can apply to your cam modeling career. More importantly, we'll focus on the specifics to a beginner's success!

TOKENS

If you're completely new to the industry, there's a good chance you haven't heard of tokens before. Tokens are a unit value that users use on the site that represents cash. Users can purchase a certain amount of tokens with their real-world money and tip performers. This is much like when people visit arcades or funfairs and convert their cash into tickets or tokens to put into machines or redeem prizes.

In the cam world, tokens are used by fans who tip you during your performance. They can either tip you to reward you for your performance or to request to see something specific. The token rates depend on the website. The more tokens somebody tips you, the more money you will earn and, consequently, improve your ranking on the list of cam girls or your status.

How to Earn Tokens

You're probably less concerned about the origin of these tokens and are looking for ways to earn tokens once you sign up on one of the best cam sites out there. So, what does

a webcam girl need to do to earn as many tokens as possible?

- Maintain a positive attitude and be authentic
- Prepare valuable accessories and tools you can use during your performance
- Listen to your audience and find out what is important to them
- Try to change up your performances and bring something new to the table
- Pay attention to your chat while performing
- Know how and when to take fans to a paid private show

How to Get Viewers into a Private Show

Private shows are where you will be able to earn a large sum of money, but you likely need to put on an enticing show that lasts a relatively long time. To achieve this, you should always treat your fans with kindness, flirt with them, and make them feel special. Keep in mind that your audience is looking for someone to provide them with a welcome escape from everyday life, have a little fun, and enjoy someone's company.

However, this doesn't mean you should pressure them into taking you to a private show. Instead, make sure everything feels natural to them by encouraging and motivating them to go to a private room. Once you get them there, you will have to maintain their attention through allure.

Whether it's by teasing them and showing off parts of your body or talking to them in a certain way, you should aim to make a connection with your fans and make them feel as if they are interacting with you in person and not via a camera.

The biggest tips will be given by those who regularly visit you every day, which means the effort for establishing that connection is incredibly valuable. Once you charm them, they will come back for more time and time again.

WHAT IS A WEBCAM MODEL'S INCOME LIKE?

Compared to other jobs, a cam girl will not be able to know how much money she will make tomorrow, in three months, or three years. Your income will be varied and sometimes unstable. You can perform at your best, stay online for long periods of time, try out various cam girl personas, but nothing will ensure a fixed income.

The key is patience. Building your audience is not easy and takes time. Use your time online to get to know your fans so you can profit from giving them exactly what they are looking for. When it comes to your potential income, it requires a bit of planning and understanding. As a beginner, you should set your prices accordingly and set goals.

- Each site has a specific dollar amount for the tokens you earn. For example, on Chaturbate, 1 token has a conversation rate of $0.05 USD. If you accumulate 1000 tokens in a show, you earn 50 dollars.
- For private shows, you can decide on the minimum number of minutes and the rate you charge per minute. If you charge a minimum of 10 minutes and set your rate to 60 tokens a minute, you will earn at least $30 USD.

Besides your audience, there are a lot of factors that affect your salary, from egirl outfits to how many hours you choose to work. For instance, if you've tried working in the afternoons and you don't seem to bring in many viewers, try working in the evenings or mornings. The first few months of your camming experience should serve as a test of what works and what doesn't. This is why you shouldn't instantly draw conclusions about your income or your number of fans. Just keep experimenting and working hard and it will pay off!

YOUR FIRST CAM SESSIONS

If you have your profile set up and you're ready to perform, but you're struggling to get viewers to click on your thumbnail and watch your show, what do you do? After all, you're new to the site and there are girls who have worked on the website for months or years. So, do you make your first few sessions more effective?

1. Before your first show, **watch other girls on the site you've signed up for**. Pay attention to girls of all popularity levels and look at what works and what doesn't. Try networking with other camgirls on social media platforms like Twitter by contacting them with your cam username. These girls can promote you by sharing your room link with their audience or advertising you on their social media accounts.

2. Some cam sites will give a **temporary visibility boost for new girls**. Research what type of boost your site offers and make the most of it. For instance, you may have a special "New" tag on your first week, so it would be a smart move to stream as much as you can during those seven days.

3. **Brainstorm ideas** about things you can do that are interesting and unique. You never know what people will be intrigued by or want to watch. Your list can

include things such as dancing, singing, crazy masks, costumes, acting, drawing on your body, or other creative and dynamic performance ideas. Just keep in mind that things that other girls don't have or do could be the most profitable thing for you.

TIPS FOR ENGAGING YOUR VIEWERS

You've done all of the above and your first show was more or less a success. Now you have all these questions about how to engage those viewers and ensure they come back, right? Well, the answer is pretty simple - be positive, interesting, attentive, energetic, and creative. Keep all of your interactions natural and authentic to you.

Don't fall into the trap of thinking you are the queen of the site because you might forget about your fans and their needs and be unprepared for when your novelty wears out. A great webcam girl knows how to put on entertaining shows to a wide audience. Maybe you don't have all the right answers on how to become an egirl which consistently attracts an audience all the time, but that's not important at this point.

Focusing on an egirl aesthetic, fun camming activities, cam site benefits, and an audience profile is the first step to building a successful cam girl career. Everything else will fall in place if you do things right from the start. If Rome wasn't built in a day, cam girls need time to build up an empire too.

How to Get More Followers on Chaturbate, Stripchat & Other Cam Sites

It's one thing to have lots of people in your room enjoying your show and another to have recurring viewers who eventually become your loyal audience. They are crucial to your success as they are not only the ones who pay for your services but the ones who determine which direction your cam career will go. If you're wondering how to become an egirl who has the knowledge and skill to build up a long-term audience, look no further because we have all the information you need.

From understanding your audience profile to determining your strengths, there are a lot of things you'll need to keep an eye out for to make sure you truly utilize your best qualities. Don't hesitate to give your all so you can build up an audience who is as ecstatic about your performances, if not more, than you!

YOUR AUDIENCE PROFILE

After you've started off on one of the best camming sites on the web, you'll gradually notice that there are thousands of other girls with the same goals. This means that you'll have to stand out from the crowd and attract people who will become repeat customers. Is there a type of audience you want to aim to lure in once you start broadcasting? How will this determine your cam girl persona and the activities you prepare for your viewers?

When thinking about selling any type of service, understanding who your audience is and what their preferences are will determine the outcome. After your first few shows, start analyzing the types of viewers you attract to determine what will likely keep them coming back. What they have in common, what they enjoy, and how they communicate with you—all of this will help you develop your cam personality and focus on the activities which will benefit you.

Write down all the things you notice about your viewers, e.g. their age, communication style, desires, what captures their attention, etc. You can even develop audience personas and start thinking about different shows you can put on to satisfy their needs, values, and desires. This will help you tremendously to deliver exactly what they are looking for.

For example, if your fans express their love for comic books, you could think about buying shirts with comic characters on it or dress up as a popular superhero like Wonder Woman, Jean Grey, or Harley Quinn.

BEST HOT CAM GIRL TRICKS

Now that you've analyzed your viewers, let's focus on some tips that will bring in the cash. After all, a cam girl needs to have some tricks up her sleeve.

Personal Connection

People look for different things on cam sites, but one thing that all viewers look for is a personal connection. Your fans want to connect with you on a personal level and feel as though they are important to you and part of your daily life.

Giving them a little peek into your room on a screen doesn't offer them that level of interaction.

To negate the feeling of physical distance, start building close relationships with them. When you are talking to your audience, it's crucial to look them in the eye (in this case, at the webcam) and make them feel significant to you. Ask them about their day, what they personally enjoy, and remember things about each user.

When you interact with them next time, ask them how that work project is going, whether they were able to purchase the car they mentioned the other day, or how they spent their birthday last week. Remember, nothing will make them feel more important than showing them you remember something about them and want to hear more about their life.

Fantasy

Besides being a part of your everyday life, there will be viewers who are looking to escape their daily life and jump into a fantasy world with you. This type of audience persona doesn't want to talk about real-life issues and simply wants to have fun. That's where you come in! Make them smile, keep things interesting, and be that casual girl that every man wants to have around.

To provide your fans with a fantasy world, you will need to get into character and pull them into that world. Make sure your efforts are natural, as forcing something and being ungenuine might result in losing your audience.

Fantasy mainly means an escape from reality but there is a more literal definition to acknowledge. It's no secret that the world of camming is populated by themes that are considered to be taboo. While outlandish, the majority of fetishes and kinks out there are not morally objectionable.

Take the time to do some research into some of these themes to find out if there are any that align with interests of yours so you can capitalize on your comfort and familiarity with the topics.

Many audience members will be incredibly generous with their wallets if they find their interest in you, especially since they normally have to seek it out or make detailed requests. If you get lucky and land on the right fantasy, that will turn into a lasting income source during your time as an Egirl.

The message here is to be open minded, and let go of reservations that might lead you to come off condescending towards certain desires. Just like acting forced, this will put a black mark on your record as a cam model.

Power Play

There is no stronger aphrodisiac than power, right? Luckily, not even technology can stand in the way of implementing power into your shows. If your fans are into power play, there are two ways you can play it out. The first one relies on you to be dominant and possess all the power where your viewers need to follow your rules if they want to take part.

The second one will create the opposite scenario. Your audience will possess the control and you will have to do whatever they ask of you. For this to work out, you may need to be a little more experienced in the cam world. It requires knowing how to control your viewers but allowing them to believe they are controlling you. So, if you want to spice things up, try out the first option and once you feel more comfortable in your role, try the second one.

The Domina genre is an avenue that pays even while you're not working but it does take a mental investment. The types of customers that seek out women who fulfill this role seldom go for a one time experience and more often want slightly deeper and longer lasting bonds.

You will have to remember each one's preferences and what you have done in past interactions to keep up the fantasy for them and not risk losing them as a customer. If you falter, there is a chance that word will spread about your inexperience and you will have a hard time getting your footing back. Women with naturally dominant personalities who are more than comfortable with their confidence will thrive in this niche.

If it feels too forced for you, you will be better off finding a different element that suits you and therefore making money will be easier in the long run. This is really a sort of pass or fail persona to embody, but do not fret! While it seems like some Domina women just sit back and rake in the cash, this is a possibility for every type of cam girl, which is why it's such a popular field!

START WITH YOURSELF

Although it is really important that you know and understand your audience, you shouldn't go out of your way to please them. You should feel comfortable with everything you do in front of the camera, so if something doesn't feel right, stop doing it. Confidence is crucial to your success, and doing things that aren't on par with who you are might decrease that level of self-esteem that your audience loves.

What you first need to learn is how to become a cam girl who knows what she wants and values and then start delivering that to your fans. What will make this entire experience more interesting and fun for *you,* and not just for the viewers? Is there something you want to try out but haven't had a chance to before? Be yourself - that's the only way for you to succeed!

You Are The Product

In line with this philosophy is the idea of investing in yourself. Modeling online can be a lucrative way to earn money and many girls earn more than enough to cover their basic expenses. Once you have your footing, it will pay off a lot to siphon some of those funds back towards you. This can look first and foremost like pampering yourself but it's very good for business. Regular hair or nail appointments, getting your lashes done, and buying quality makeup will end up paying for itself when your appearance and confidence sends fans to your page in droves.

Let's break this down a little. Egirls all keep different schedules, this is the beauty of being one, but you will probably end up spending several hours at a time on camera. Wearing cheap makeup for hours at a time, or not having the right cleanser to wash it off when you are done, can lead to breakouts, which pushes your audience away either by your appearance or your lack of assurance in yourself. Don't skimp on this area and invest in high quality products to protect your moneymaker.

This next avenue is a more literal path to revenue. If you have the tenacity for it, keeping well manicured toes can attract a selection of high paying followers that are known for their strong preferences and will pay good money to keep seeing individuals who possess their favorite type of tootsies.

Prioritizing yourself and your appearance by outsourcing the upkeep will also contribute to the image you should be trying to project as a cam girl. Sure you can save a little money by cutting your own hair and painting your nails at home but you need to start thinking of your time as money. The time that you spend in your own bathroom doing the work can be spent in the salon chair on your phone handling your social media presence. Patrons of cam girls also want to be supporting the idea of a carefree, desirable, and sometimes just out of reach woman. Creating as many elements that support that image as possible will help maintain the fantasy for them and add up in small ways down the line.

Playing Dress Up

Once this initial personal investment starts helping you bring home the bacon, you will have even more funds to redirect to yourself so you can boost your income further. When you first started you probably only had one or two sets of lingerie you could change into for your more private shows.

Now is the perfect time to buy a few more, obtain a variety to see what both you and your fans prefer, and even opt for high quality specialty pieces that only the lucky few get the chance to see you in. Included in this category are tights, thigh high socks, and fishnets, as well as statement jewelry pieces and shoes.

Speaking of shoes, these are a great and simple money earner with audience members who will want to make specific requests (for a price) to see you strut your stuff in a particular set of heels. If you have a love for beautiful shoes, you can build up your personal collection this way, either with the money you earn or by allowing lucky fans to purchase pairs for you to perform in for one on one shows.

If you're indifferent about pumps, just invest in a few good pairs that meet a wide range of desires. Red bottom stilettos, leather or latex boots, and clear platform dancer heels are great starting places.

Creating Your Space

The final level of self investment extends beyond you a little bit, but it's your space and any "tools" you might be using to make your job more lucrative and fun! Consider where you are filming. Is it in your bedroom on your bed? A luxurious bed set upgrade can really boost your environment and attract higher paying viewers who enjoy a glamorous camgirl experience.

If you work from another room or space, strongly consider what your viewers see and can infer about your life from their observations and take control of that perspective to work in your favor.

Any furniture should be clean and updated, if the angle of your camera placement can't be adjusted and you can see more of your home than is needed, consider buying a decorative room divider to make the space more intimate and free from distractions. This will also improve sound quality.

One way that cam girls make a lot of money through investing in themselves is by performing with toys. Fans love to participate in this form of intimacy and will spend longer amounts of time in private paid chats when toys are involved.

Many Egirls prefer to keep their personal toys and the ones they use to perform separate but this is based on preference and not a requirement, especially when you are first starting out. Keep in mind though, that the toys you enjoy on your own and the kind that are more theatrically appealing for cam shows might be a bit different.

Male fans might prefer to see themselves represented in your toys versus pink or purple glittery representations. A great way to give the fans what they want is to let your more loyal return members purchase and send you items off a wishlist and they pay to see you perform with their selection. This can also help you build up your collection quickly!

KEEP THEM COMING BACK

Knowing how to become an egirl that brings in loyal customers is not easy, but if you come up with a strategy and stay true to who you are, there's a good chance people will come back for more. One of the best ways to ensure people will come back is by mentioning what might happen in your next show. For instance, if you're thinking about doing a special fantasy show for your audience, announce and promote that across social media and during your show.

The key is to treat all of your cam sessions like a collective instead of a one-off. Use your performance to tell a story and find the most engaging ways to convert your viewers into repeat customers. Make them happy on your online platforms whether it is by chatting with them on your social media or performing specific shows for them on cam.

Another way to keep the money ball rolling in this industry is through a series of side hustles. Many popular cam girls create a following that is more than happy to pay to get just a little bit closer. Selling personal items of yours is a distanced way to create this illusion of closeness.

This can be done really easily too and can be worked into your shows. Simply buy additional pairs of socks, stockings, tights, and even underwear that you wear in your shows or day to day and then make them available for sale.

You won't believe the market for these kinds of items, and there are even third party sites that handle the shipping and ordering process for you. Items can increase in price depending on how long they are worn and even for specialty activities like worn at the gym or worn overnight.

Another side hustle involves keeping alternate socials. Many cam girl sites take a cut of the price you set per minute with your customers. These sites are excellent ways to build up a following, but once you are comfortable, it's entirely possible to create your own content offsite and have customers pay you directly.

For example, many online performers offer access to a premium snapchat account where customers pay either a one time or monthly fee for access to stories, direct messages, and photos and videos by following you on snapchat.

Thanks to privacy settings, you can control who is following you at any time and keep a record of who has paid their dues to join your exclusive club.

CONCLUSION

Here is a list of some great ways a webcam girl can engage her audience and keep viewers coming back:

- Post photos and videos to your social media channels.
- Do teasers before going live and make sure your audience knows you're going online.
- During your show, let your viewers know where they can find more of you on the Internet e.g. Instagram, Facebook, or YouTube.
- Create your own loyalty program for customers. It can include anything from an emoji next to their name to a monthly video call or winning a photo set.
- Play off your cam girl persona and create your own signature looks and theme. Nothing is off-limits!
- Don't focus solely on the money. Creating an unforgettable experience and a fun environment will make your job more exciting and keep your audience engaged. The money will come naturally.

While the average model cams for 18 hours per week and makes just over $1,000 from doing so, models who cam for **35+ hours per week** typically make **$2,500 per week** or more.

On the lower end, models who cam for 5 to 10 hours per week tend to make only around

$350 per week.

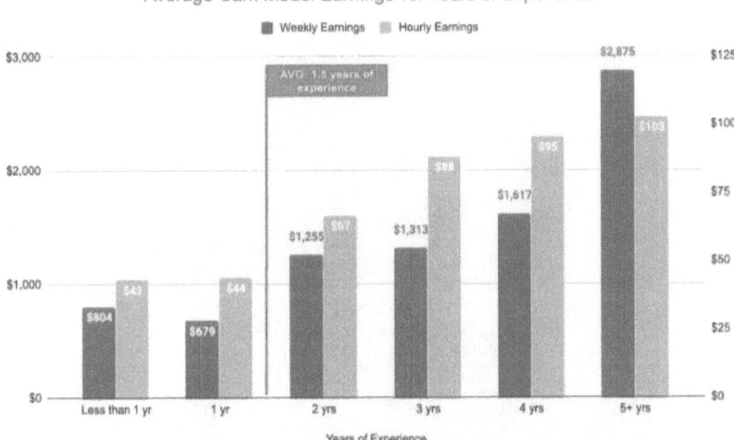

One of the more powerful takeaways from this data is just how viable webcam modeling is as a full-time career. While most only cam part-time, the webcam models who treat it as a full-time profession make over **$136,500 per year** on average. That's nearly twice the median household income in the United States!

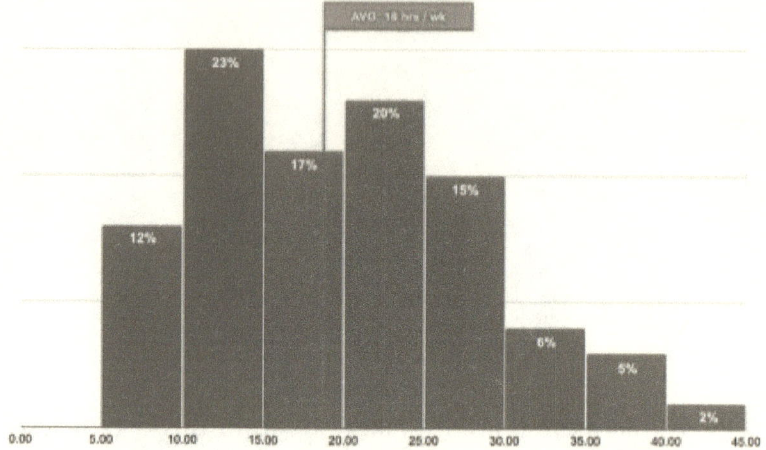

How Much Time Models Spend Camming in a Typical Week
AVG 16 hrs / wk
23%
20%
17%
15%
12%
6%
5%
2%
0.00
5.00
10.00
15.00
20.00
25.00
30.00
35.00
40.00
45.00

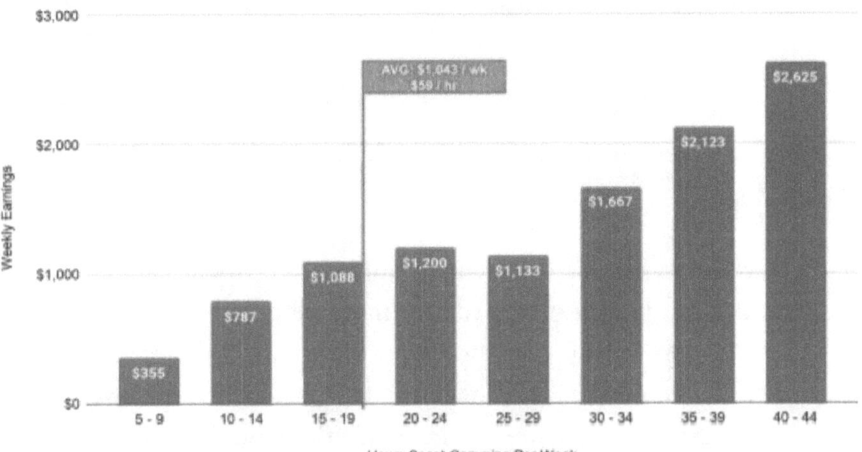

Hours Worked	**Earnings Per Week**	**Earnings Per Month**	**Earnings Per Year**
5 hrs / wk	$355	$1,521	$18,511
10 hrs / wk	$787	$3,373	$41,036
15 hrs / wk	$1,088	$4,663	$56,731
25 hrs / wk	$1,133	$4,856	$59,078
20 hrs / wk	$1,200	$5,143	$62,571
30 hrs / wk	$1,667	$7,144	$86,922
35 hrs / wk	$2,123	$9,099	$110,699
40+ hrs / wk	$2,625	$11,250	$136,875

Average Salary For Different Broadcaster Types

The final analysis we'll be providing in this report is how earnings varies for webcam models based on the type of broadcaster they are (e.g. Female vs. Male vs. Trans vs. Couples).

Overall, we found that female broadcasters spent the most time camming, and earned the most per hour on average, resulting in female cam models earning nearly double what their male peers make. Female models earn **$1,093 per week** on average, or **$61 per hour**, while male models earn just **$409 per week** on average, or **$33 per hour**.

Trans broadcasters came in at #2, with earnings nearly as high as female broadcasters on average, at **$940 per week** and **$50 per hour**.

Based on our survey data, couples seem to spend less time camming than any other broadcaster type, and earn just **$205 per week** or **$35 per hour** on average.

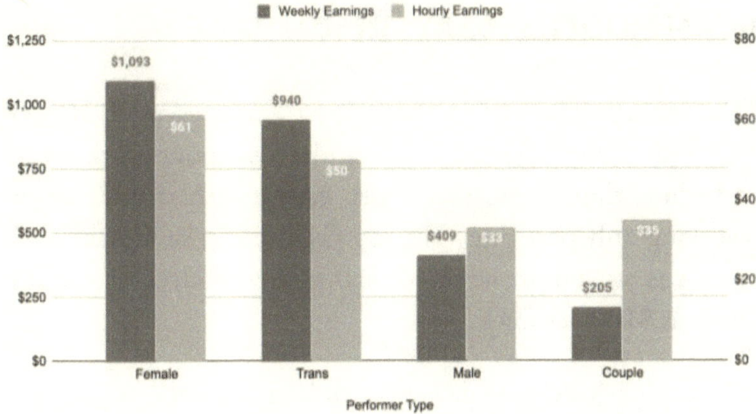

Average Cam Model Earnings by Performer Type
Weekly Earnings
Hourly Earnings
$1,250
$1,000
$750
$500
$250
$0
$80
$60
$40
$20
$0
$1,093
$61
$940
$50
$409
$33
$205
$35
Female
Trans
Male
Couple
Performer Type

WEBCAM MODEL SALARY - IN SUMMARY

The average cam girl in the United States earns $136,500 per year when adjusted to a standard 40 hour work week schedule, though most cam girls earn less than this due to working only part-time. The top professional models earn as much as $6,000 per week, while beginner models can earn as little as $100 per week.

How much a webcam makes depends on a number of factors, including:

1. Which cam site they use
2. How many hours they work
3. How long they've been camming for
4. How good they are at entertaining their audience
5. Ability to build loyal followers

Cam Girl Hourly Pay

Based on the survey results, most experienced cam models (with 3 yrs of experience or more) earn between $80 - $200 per hour. A cam girl with this level of experience can take home as much as $1,000 from a full 8-hour day. Most cam models choose to work less than a full 8-hour day on average though, so earnings for a typical cam model are more like $300 per day for 2-4 hours of work.

Beginner cam models (1 year of experience or less) earn between $40-$50 per hour on average. Models with a medium level of experience (around 2 yrs) tend to earn roughly $60-$70 per hour.

How Much Should I Expect To Make From Camming?

The amount of money you make will depend on various factors we covered above such as your experience, clientele, ability to charm your viewers, the type of broadcaster you are, and how much time you dedicate to broadcasting.

Like any job, as a webcam model you will experience ups and downs. In particular, you'll experience it with income. Some days you'll be well-paid very quickly, and others you may only earn a few dollars for a long day's work (especially when starting out). The important thing is that you prepare yourself for the best and the worst.

Should you quit your job immediately and start working solely as a cam girl? Maybe, maybe not—that decision is up to you. However, make sure you use all the free time you have to learn more about being a cam girl and how to use all of the tools and resources available to you.